A FAE STATE STORY

TALES OF FAEJA & JAFAE

JAMES MULLEN III

PAGE PUBLISHING
Conneaut Lake, PA

First originally published by Page Publishing 2024

ISBN 979-8-89315-907-3 (pbk)
ISBN 979-8-89315-920-2 (digital)

Printed in the United States of America

CONTENTS

Prologue...v

The Opening Page 1

A Fae Origin Story 3

A Rare Glimpse...6

A Holiday Tale 9

Source-Coder Colony.......................................13

The Woodland Elves 16

Ogham Assassin Training 18

Space Battle Commander 21

Battlefield Elves...24

FAE Prime..30

FAE Christianity 33

Archcardinal Orenda 34

The Crusades 35

A Wizard's Ambush 38

1588...41

How the Revolutionary War Was Won...........44

American FAE...48

A Kandyland Story...50

Along the Journey 58

Afterward 61

An Elf on the Shelf..65

PROLOGUE

There is little and less written and left over than there should be about the FAE in our common era we find ourselves in today. Often called the Others or the Fair Folk, the FAE come from the Elder lineage, the first species to develop and adapt. Surviving age after age, they still live in nearby parallels and other worlds and walk hidden among you. The Others are people that still cross back and forth from this world through various ways.

From this perspective, what we consider FAE includes the following: the Pale FAE deities and Treefolk Shape-shifters, the Tan and Pale FAE, elves, leprechauns, and some dragons.

The FAE were the first and most important and still exist yet remain largely forgotten and unseen. FAE time works differently for immortals and Elders, and one feels enhanced when around the FAE. There are also many erased and altered histories of what once was and still remains.

These were fairy-tale stories, a collection of histories from this world and others, from our multiverse and beyond, and this is Book 1. I hope you enjoy and possibly learn and expand your perception of what has been and what might be and consider what's still not yet revealed.

THE OPENING PAGE

For this was a blender world, a book's and story world, with a TV and movie overlay, an old war parallel, and a study, observation, and experimental world as well.

I was an Elder Reviewer of many different things. Wherever my attention took me, I was allowed to review. For I was Pale FAE JAFAE!

I achieved mastery over life and death long ago; many lives now passed by. When I die and begin anew, I re-materialize my Takeon field and bring myself back into manifest form. As Pale FAE JAFAE, I renew and insert myself into the compatible resonant world or domain or dimension where I am needed, each time through my pure form of authentic being or a hidden integrator avatar, whatever works for the mission that's needed in a given security sector.

I existed in this world before time began from another FAE dimensional multiverse. As Pale FAE JAFAE, I exist as my intrinsic identity. After training in FAE psychology, I created FAE STATE Private Sector. Using FAE STATE design, I've created many things and destroyed many things too, but that's a whole different story still not revealed, you know.

What has been is being remembered through all that we do. Through our thoughts, words, and actions, we create, sustain, destroy, and perceive awakened anew.

This book needs to be written, the whole thing, even if only for me, to process my thoughts and experiences.

Writers like to speak aloud and hear what their writing sounds like, a self-read conversation with creative prose. It's part of the process: to write and rewrite and edit and find clarity in the message. The more I write, the better I feel as I put pen and ink on the page. The information flows forth, and that's for the best, for truth is far stranger than fiction.

I play on many levels of existence, but I operate small on tokens away from the higher vibrational planes. Through parallel worlds, I travel into many different domains.

There was a story to be told, a tale to tell, and on and on it goes, the chapters of my life remembered, written, and shared—foretold. This phase of my existence along with my Elderverse goes much farther than you know. From the deepest depths within, Source Codes are remembered and renewed.

Prophecy through preception, the future is partially perceived— signs and symbols and synchronicity, a true reality seen through the mind.

Early in the night, long before the morning, I continue to write by candlelight the way it used to be. Pen and paper, ideas flow forth, sharing the story of JAFAE.

A FAE ORIGIN STORY

Originally I was a Source Coder named James, from the Source Origin, and was Tan FAE. But I wanted to be more. So I chose, from the many manifest forms, a perfect template blend. I chose to be who I wanted above all else to become and evolve into, and my choice was paramount into all I would become and perceive through. So I chose to be a Treefolk Shape-shifter, and I incarnated within a vast race of Treefolk Shape-shifters. But both rare and possible, I was born with three species templates already built in—my secret choice. I was all three, a Pale FAE, Elf, and Treefolk, and could shape-shift between all three species variations.

At once, I was placed in Treeschool on a lifelong Ogham training with all the other Treefolk Shape-shifter children. After a short while, I really stood out and was selected by the female rulers and Treeschool Trainers to become Treefolk king TreeFAE. As king TreeFAE, I sat the Treefolk throne for one million years and reigned supreme, with guidance from female shape-shifter Treefolk rulers, who still exist to this very day, being Elders themselves, my Elders. As I sat the throne in my Treefolk form as TreeFAE, I peered and used inner vision to look into the far futures of my many lives and shape-shift variations. But I discovered that I would eventually become FAEJA, Treeja, and Nevele, that I had turned myself into a FAEmosis, Treemosis, and Elfmosis, and that I would live out female incarnations as well as shape-shift between them.

Eventually, one million years passed by, and my service and duty as Treefolk Shape-shifter king had come to a completion. So with the blessings of my Treefolk Elders, the female conclave, TreeFAE chose a new dimension to live in, where he could be both JAFAE AND FAEJA as a FAEmosis, Pale FAE, both shape-shifting into male and female, living with other Pale FAE around a New Life Generator of a FAE design, from another private sector, older than mine.

Here enters Bob and Fiona into this story, a Pale FAEmosis themselves. Bob, the Builder, designed and built FAE and Elemental New Life Generators that brought new beings to life. And that's where I existed among other Pale FAE so we could develop ourselves in our new species variation, both as FAEJA and JAFAE. We lived with that group of Pale FAE for a long, long time, safe in numbers and hidden from view, with new Pale FAE being generated each year into fresh new life. The trick is at first I pretended I came from the generator too and that I was a FAEmosis like our creator Bob the Builder and his Fiona. So the Pale FAE community allowed FAEJA and JAFAE to stay as long as they liked, as long as necessary. For it was an all-male community of FAE that lived and guarded the New Life Generator. All the female Pale FAE were welcomed to life and then given guidance or places to go and then sent on their way, never to return. That was their custom. Even as FAEJA, not once did any of the males mate with her, although she deeply desired it and wanted too. She was told not to look for special attention from the FAE males.

After thousands of years, it was time once again to experience ourselves as a new species variation. So FAEJA as Nevele, calling herself Diana, incarnated in an Elven sequence of lives and, in her first of these, becomes a queen of the elves. She ruled well and kept her own council until she was raped and murdered by the Elf psychologist who then made himself king in her place. Later, Nevele incarnated through several short Elf lives, and in the last of the sequence with her signature, orange Elf hair was a battle captain in the Elven military and an Elven majick user. Through Elven majick, she earned a noble title as countess. She also applied to train as a psychologist but was denied. Not much later, she came into danger, and there were elves who wanted to kill her, and she remembered in a time of need her FAEmosis JAFAE existing within her always and immediately shape-shifted into her masculine self. JAFAE, fresh to life, quickly killed off all one hundred elves, securing the perimeter and elimi-nating all threats nearby and eliminating everyone else in the small Elven nation very quickly as a Pale FAE moved. This freed FAEJA Nevele from any and all Elf contracts and bindings from that place and people, now that they no longer existed, and there were many lives we have lived, in many places, in many timelines, and in many worlds and multiverses.

This is our FAE STORY, of JAFAE, TreeFAE, and James, as well as FAEJA, Treeja, and Nevele. So the story unfolds. We were a fairy-tale creature.

A RARE GLIMPSE

As far as we remember from what has been experienced and recorded, we recollect the beginning. What created them we will never know. There were once many mega beings with various faces, they could rotate their persona from one to the next, depending on their moods. Within themselves they had all the species templates for civilization to set down and create but with the intention to destroy it all; everything brought to life was planned for annihilation. They were dark and demented creatures with no love or joy for that which they could create.

First, they set forth the Tan FAE Source Coders. Early original templates were created and brought to life. But the Tan FAE were highly intelligent as well as telepathic. They read the minds of mega beings that they were going to kill them all not long after they were brought forth through conscious creation.

The FAE fought back, every one of them, in the thousands and slaughtered mega beings with their rotted intentions, thus, freeing themselves and all future creation from the overlord mega beings.

The Tan FAE Source Coders had the ability and responsibility to set forth existence after that, now being responsible for all future species templates and Source Codes that would be set down into conscious creation, and there was a near unlimited species variation and potential to be brought into existence.

First, they chose the FAE, the first species, the Elder lineage. They set forth the Pale FAE deities, who could bring other FAE varieties to life, and that's exactly what they perpetuated. The Pale FAE deities created first the Treefolk Shape-shifters. The Treefolk Shape-shifters immediately took a unique version of a Pale FAE deity with all their powers and abilities plus their own. The Treefolk Shape-shifters told the other deities that they were like them now, except more advanced because they were now two species and would eventually become more as well. So they went their own way perpetuating and perceiving life into existence, still thriving to this day.

Next, the Pale FAE deities created the Pale FAE, followed by the Treefolk, elves, leprechauns, elementals, and the first of the dragons. These were the FAE spectrum of life, varied and diverse as they are.

First came the FAE, and then came the nightcrawlers crawling through the dark matter. But they weren't enemies. In fact, the Venom Elite still coordinate with the Treefolk for missions to this very day. Then each species was set down one after the other; the chosen order long forgotten for most species stopped existing long ago, and that's for the best, making room for younger species while the Elder FAE still maintain their ancestral domains and dimensions, those they can hold and defend.

Of the original world spectrums set forth, the first were nature filled on Ogham with lots of Treefolk and elves. The next were Kandyland worlds, thousands alongside core planets among them. The planets were brightly colorful, dangerous, and strangely made of candy. With a multitude of Kandyland species, very varied in form and capability, they were the first military, and there are many legends of the great Kandyland wars. Kandyland is still thriving in this era in the FAE dimensions.

This was the Elder way and lineage I come from as FAEJA and JAFAE, Nevele and James, Treeja and TreeFAE, first as a Source Coder and then a Treefolk Shape-shifter, becoming all three—Pale FAE, Treefolk, and an Elven Elf. Later we become FAE deity as well with Christmas elves. These original templates from the Source Origin still exist in the form of the original Elders and their creations in manifest form. The memory of the Elderverse is the proper way.

> And many species had come before…like the Elders FAE, Treefolk, and Elves, original templates of the many multiverses. And many dan-

gerous creatures had arrived as well later on. And we fought them in the darkness and we fought them in the light, and we hid and waited and watched from the shadows, and that was our delight.

A HOLIDAY TALE

In the beginning, before time began, there was a great and massive war over religious holidays, in which one was the most important. Most dominant during the era were the Scarecrow elves who celebrated Halloween and Christmas elves who celebrated Christmas. Eventually, as the war played itself out, the Christmas elves pulled forward with their tenacity, vigor, and weaponry. Although the scarecrow elves could fly and levitate and utilized scarecrow alchemy against their opponents, the Christmas elves were very fast and larger in numbers, with blaster rifles each shooting the scarecrows down from the sky.

Calling a truce and recognizing both holidays as sacred and worth celebrating to this day, they each celebrate the other's main holiday, both Christmas and Halloween. Sadly though, as a fallout of these early wars over religion, most elves have banned religious practice altogether as well as holy days. But because of the specific variation of the species, both Christmas and Scarecrow elves still observe and celebrate in their own ways these FAE Elven holidays.

"It's time to incarnate again," I said to myself. The region and species had been looked over and chosen. "I will incarnate with the elves again and be an Elven male as James once more."

The parents I incarnated with were royalty from two different elf tribes, small rural nations. They consorted together, mating vigorously, and the female conceived me as a child. Shortly after, I was born on the solstice, in a white winter wilderness, with snow everywhere. The women presented the small Elf child to the father, but both decided to abandon the baby in the snow, unattended, cold, and alone. Shortly thereafter, I died, which only took a few hours. I slipped away from life easily in those conditions but still exist formless, hovering near where I had last breathed life. After three days, I reformed into a physical form, returning as young JAFAE the Elder. In my Pae FAE manifestation, I could fly and levitate and was not susceptible to the frigid cold. I was happy to be alive and Pale FAE again. Although I had planned on being Elven, I always preferred Pale FAE JAFAE, my truest self.

Wanting to move on, I flew away from the space I had been left to die, traveling deeper into the winter wilderness. Then I came across the most magnificent and beautiful brightly decorated pine tree with ornaments, garlands, and glitter and found there were a number of them.

The first person I crossed paths with was a female Christmas elf named Erika, my first friend. She welcomed me into their tribe, introduced me to everyone, and petitioned for me to be able to stay, for it was an all-female elf tribe and it was their tradition to only allow female elves in their small Christmas nation, but I was a Pale FAE; however, Erika said, "He's a sacred omen and a Christmas blessing that's just about to come to pass. Also he could fly, so we could use him to place all golden stars at the top of the Christmas pines."

The tribe voted and, with Erika's persuasion, allowed me to stay, even though I was a male FAE and they were all female elves. Later I realized we're better together, and I easily merged into the ways of the tribe. I loved their Christmas holiday, which they celebrated all year long, with special reveals in December 25 itself, different depending on the year.

Much time passed, and Erika and I became closer and closer. Eventually, she petitioned for me to become Christmas king JAFAE in their small elf nation. Everyone decided it was the right move. The first thing I did was to take Erika for my elf wife and make her the Christmas queen. I also married three other elf wives. They told me I had to choose four altogether. All beautiful, highly intelligent, and incredibly tactical—I chose well, and we lived for thousands of years together, until I eventually had to be deployed elsewhere. Even then, I still came back for marital visits before the marriages become annulled.

Christmas elves were incredibly intelligent and excellent at making things, especially toys and advanced weaponry, especially glitter guns. I appreciated Erika more and more as our marriage and rule deepened. Eventually, she showed me how to become a Pale FAE deity, what the species are and what they represent, how they were the first species set forth by the Source Coders, and how they could bring other FAE, Elven, Treefolk, and elementals to life anew. This was what she wanted for me, for us, and our small nation.

So after we made love, with deep thrusts and multiple orgasms, each we went outside our dwelling, and I leveled up into a Pale FAE deity for the first time, truly becoming the Christmas king, James Christmas, as young JAFAE. I shape-shifted into a tall male with wide shoulders and a lean waist and sharp teeth. I became stronger than ever with strange new powers and abilities. Erika then gave me a traditional red Christmas hat with a jingle bell on the end to wear and make my outfit compete. She then became Saint Erika, the Christmas queen and patron saint of Christmas.

Sometimes, my wives would capture me in a rolling office chair, tie me up with colored ribbon, and spin me around in circles, laughing all the while. Then they would release me, so I would scream and chase them. This would get them off, and they would have so much fun. Then we would have great sex together. My wives are the only four Christmas Elves in the tribe that I mated with, and that was our way.

Sometimes, on Christmas, when the veils between the realms would grow thin, we would sail our Elven airships through the sky to another parallel world, fully armed and ready to attack and explore, but not every year.

We also celebrated Halloween once each year, taking a small break from the yearly cheery Christmas celebrations. We liked to keep it spooky, so we would tell all kinds of species stories from our Elven and FAE race memories around orange shellacked pumpkins.

Christmas elves would come trick-or-treating on Christmas, and Scarecrow elves would bring presents on Halloween (you know you're deep in the story now)—what a blend that is and would be again. So keep a watchful eye out, for the Elders still exist, waiting and watching for the right moment to reveal themselves once more.

> The Scarecrow elves out at night, they cause a
> fright, for their utter delight.
> On Halloween, levitating and patiently watching
> costumed children collecting candy.
> Keep it spooky! Orange pumpkins, black cats, all
> on Halloween.
> And put an elf on your shelf at Christmas, along-
> side your Christmas tree.

SOURCE-CODER COLONY

O nce I was a little Tan FAE boy who incarnated into life with noble parents, on a Source-Coder space colony. My mother was regal, beautiful, and strong. She was a duchess and was combat tested having killed before in battle. My father was a brutal murderer, a count who killed off everyone in our colony.

Most days I would follow my mother around, trailing not too far behind, and watch her beautiful bottom, her bum from behind, with a smile. She would always take me on the bridge, having the highest security clearance to gain access. On the bridge they grew multiverses and chose species in order by world age and era to populate them in the experimental chosen charts. These were a very advanced and very well-practiced special research colony of Tan FAE Source Coders.

The bridge was always guarded by the sentinels, armed and ready, always prepared. "Hoodly hey," I would say to them, and "Hoodly who," they would respond in greeting. We would say "Hoodles" for short to one another in greeting as we walked along the colony walkways, my mother and me smiling behind.

One day, I heard my parents arguing, so I left my room to see what was happening. Just in time, I saw the count struck the duchess in the head with a club, smashing her dead as she dropped to the ground. My murderous father, the count, had already taken control of the sentinels that guard the colony and who were completely loyal to him and no longer protect our colonists. I ran for the bridge, sprinting past my room, knowing the count will kill me next if I let him. Tears poured down my face at the loss of my mother. I reached the hallway by the bridge and hid in the housekeeping closet, behind the boxes, buckets, mops, and brooms. Days passed by, and slowly everyone on the Source-Coder Colony was picked off, one by one, a club to the head, a smash, and a crash as the bodies fall to the floor, many more until everyone was gone.

Gaining confidence, I began to study and alter the main multiverse, growing and coding experiments on each unfinished project. I changed as much as I could for each new multiverse being grown and expanded, I rearranged the species templates set down in order, and I deleted as many dangerous species potentials as I could, permanently erasing their ability to exist in physical form.

Once I heard thunderous footsteps and father rambling to himself aloud once again, "Little boy, little boy, where are you hiding? I'm going to kill you next!" So I ran to the housekeeping closet just at the end of the hall on the bridge and hid inside the closet, concealed in the back of the room. The footsteps stopped outside the room, and then I heard him speak once more, "I should have left some people alive just to clean this place up last time before I gave them the smash with my club to the head." Then there was a pause in silence before I heard him walk loudly away.

The next morning, I came out and about from my hiding place in the housekeeping closet and knew I had to get away. I needed to escape through one of the experimental projects, so I opened a small portal as Pale FAE JAFAE and flew through space very far away.

I had been working on a completely untapped multiverse sector, just beginning to grow and expand, of the species available already chosen. I had full access to arrange them in template order of existence, and these were the first I chose from our shared multiverse we live in now: a Scarecrow elf, a Pale FAE predator, a Treefolk, and a Venom Elite. These were the guardian template Source Codes embedded in this existence, my top choices out of what's available in the experiment. I wanted to be all of them. Eventually, I shapeshifted into all these species variations. Next, I deleted each and every dangerous species that the controls will allow, erasing life before it could begin. After that, I moved the humans away from the Orcs, until later on, in the experiment they had been chosen as a food source for Orcs, which would make them way too strong. After choosing the order of the species in this infantile multiverse, just now beginning to grow, I turned myself into a Pale FAE boy as young JAFAE and opened a doorway, jumping through and escaping the imminent death awaiting me on the Source-Coder Colony. I was a guardian and Source Coder of our multiverse because of this experimental project I inherited, and that's why I mainly resided in these realms and parallels.

Many years later, I looked up a video security footage off the security grid of the Source-Coder Colony. I was interested to know if I could find out more or if there were other known colonies that grew and populated the whole multiverses, but I never knew or found them. What I did find was security footage of the murderous count, my father, in that life for a brief while, killing off the last of the sentinels, his loyal guards. He killed them one by one and couldn't help himself and smiled when the deed was done. They got what they deserved for abandoning everyone else already. I was happy they died and that they didn't have to be on guard duty any longer.

THE WOODLAND ELVES

Once there was a small nation of Woodland elves in another dimension that I was connected with through Ogham training.

The princess had contracted a rare disease after traveling off world, and she died. I happened to be in their Elven nation at the time of her passing. The whole nation was depressed over the loss of their beloved princess.

So I shape-shifted in FAEJA as a blonde Elven female as Nevele to fill the gap and supplant the loss of their princess. They made me queen of the elves. Nevele twice visited this rural Woodland elf nation and was named queen for the time she served, hundreds of years. Both times, she took the court into the wilderness and would sing and speak in a rural Elven dialect.

She would run security perimeter checks with her seven guards all armed with spears and knives. They could run up and down the massive old, grown trees with rapid speed and heightened ability. They were very fit and agile and a happy Woodland elf species. Nevele would mate every day with her seven guardsman, and they knew how to fuck her well, into ecstatic delight. They would practice the seven-point anal penetration where each would slide their elf cock into her ass in a different direction, all seven, one after another, in quick thick succession, until they would come in her bum and the activity would be completed. This was Nevele's favorite game they played, seven-point anal penetration with her loyal elf guards each and every day. The blonde Woodland elves loved Nevele with all their spirit and knew her as a Elfmosis, as well as James. They offered him the king position, but he wanted to be an elf queen instead.

Nevele has twice ruled as rural queen of this Woodland elf nation, and both times she had the same seven guards she would mate, sing, explore, and patrol with, filling her days and feeling deeply fulfilled. She would lay naked contemplating her sequence of lives in the green grass underneath her favorite trees and agreeing with her male guards that this was the proper way to live and rule in bliss together.

Another short story of FAEJA as Nevele was as a sun-blonde, sparkly green-eyed elf this time with a horny ass and firm breasts with rock-hard nipples; her pink puss was wet to the touch at the idea of being intimate each day with her Elven honor guard. They were close, very close, and she knew she loved them all. Stronger together, this particular Woodland elf nation, although small, was very advanced, with a large city center and mostly stone buildings; everything else was spread out. That's why Nevele ruled from the wilderness, mostly thriving in nature with her honor guard.

Dreaming an Elven dream of awakening and remembrance each day anew. Until it was time to leave as James refreshed and renewed each time. The story lives on in this tale told today, all the way, on Elven time code.

> An elf would hiddenly take little sips of a nip of maple syrup by the fire at night in delight at the secret sweetness of the maple syrup, harvested through the maple trees, never telling another Elf where he finds it because if he did, they would drink it by the gallon, and then it would all be gone, and there wouldn't be a nip to sip for the elf by the fire at night in delight of the secret sweetness.

OGHAM ASSASSIN TRAINING

Once again it was time to take a female incarnation, and JAFAE was doing security work for another company when he researched that he could enter an E-L-F Ogham assassin training for female elves. Being an Elfmosis as Nevele, he applied on the Ogham network training spectrum and was accepted. Arriving in an elf dimension as Nevele, she entered the Ogham building where she would be living for the next ten years. The building was a large four-story wooden structure, secluded, and secure. Nevele entered and immediately had to give up her clothes.

"You're to remain naked for the rest of this assassin training alongside all the other female candidates. This will mean you're ready for anything and the loss of your clothes will never stop you from operating on missions and eliminating targets," she was told.

She stripped down to the nude, dropping her garments to the side. Nevele smiled standing there with her glowing green eyes and orange hair, nipples hard and firm, and breasts exposed. Nevele loved to be naked and felt comfortable in her own skin. Next, she was given a sharp curved dagger and was told everyone in the training was assigned one.

"You will keep this dagger by your side, in hand, throughout the entire training, always being armed and ready to strike and kill."

Everyone practiced with their daggers daily and carried it with them at all times. Then, Nevele was introduced to the other Ogham candidates, all female elves. Nevele was the only one with orange hair, standing out.

There were always four armed assassins guarding the inside perimeter of the locked and reinforced in the front door on the first floor. They were assigned to that position always. There were about thirty Ogham trainees in the program among the elves who have applied and been accepted. They used the security console to get updates and training tips and directives each day on Ogham training.

Time passed by swiftly. Eventually, Nevele became the head assassin and was put in charge of the Ogham base. She resided on the fourth floor now and read intelligence reports each day, from the security console to everyone else in the guild. There were five top-floor assassins, with Nevele as the leader. Each day and only for the assassins on the top floor, the top female elves, they would use the dildo to one another on through anal sex, an hour apiece. Everyone else would watch and stand guard when they're not actively participating with the female dildo sex exercises.

Eventually, a decade passed, and Nevele and her top-floor assassins graduated the program on Ogham. Then, they were sent on dangerous missions, removing their targeted marks. Ogham had a vast network and database across the many multiverses. Ogham made use of judicials, agents, and assassins to do hits wherever they need to strike. The most advanced Ogham trainers were the Treefolk themselves.

Many lifetimes later, Nevele as her Pale FAE self FAEJA with blonde hair did a follow-up assassin training, a master poisons training with the blue-lipped Pale FAE Armak. The Armak were a Pale FAE subspecies that are famous for reading and writing FAE script English backward for hidden meanings. They had blue lips because in the training and community, the Pale FAE would drink a deep-blue dye every day to increase immunity and extend their lives, thus turning their lips a light-blue color. It was quite the contrast to their pale skin tone and their wicked smiles. Only a Pale FAE could survive drinking the deep-blue dye, being highly toxic otherwise.

FAEJA, now with blue lips herself, learned many things about herself and many different types of poisons, to both kill and boost immunity, for all different types of species. FAEJA could fly and levitate, which she would do for a long time each day when not in her lessons. She was very attracted to her male mentor, being impressed with all the knowledge he had shared and his style of teaching. She wanted to mate with him, but he declined saying, "I prefer to be celibate as a Pale FAE male, although you are very attractive." This training lasted for one thousand years, and FAEJA deeply appreciated all she learned and grew to love the Pale FAE Armak male conclave she lived with and their way of life in secret study and poison practice.

They told her, "JAFAE can never undertake the blue-lipped poison training as a male FAE. That is not his destiny, but just for her." So FAEJA departed their FAE society, eager to register her updated poison assassin training on her Ogham account.

As time went on, FAEJA/Nevele worked for other intelligence agencies and continued with the Ogham network as an experienced assassin, lady-agent assassin, and lady because she was noble as well. She could mix with many circles and places and among many people, through many worlds.

SPACE BATTLE COMMANDER

As JAFAE, I was deployed in deep space for an ongoing all-out war. I was in command of a small, mid-sized spaceship with fifty immortal battle babes that I had joined up with forming my unit. Our ship was fast, spacious, and comfortable, as well as high-tech. The fifty blonde battle babes had all grown up together on an all-female planet, trained for battle since they were little girls. They knew their way around swords and knives, and we all had space battle machine guns issued to us. We would follow the ongoing war through the security network hardwired into the ships mainframe database, knowing where to travel next and where we were most vitally needed.

Each time we joined in before battle, we would land with our coordinates on a given planet and then merge in with all the newly arrived space forces, supplementing additional personnel for the already stationed ground soldiers awaiting a fresh attack. Each time, we would overwhelm the enemy position with our allied forces and heavy weaponry, achieving many victories. Afterward, we would check our gear and weaponry and then board our spaceship, leaving each world as soon as the mission was complete. We would fuck regularly as I would enter their puss from behind each time. I had excellent stamina to please and pleasure them all. Among the fifty battle babes, they kept track on who was next up for sex among them with JAFAE, and that was how we spent our space travel time in between ground assault battles. We were all experienced war veterans.

Once while aboard our spaceship, we got word that the Persian slavers down on Earth were about to conquer the known world and there was only one small kingdom that was willing and able to make a stand and fight back with a well-trained and organized standing army, Sparta, with King Leonitus and his famous three hundred at the Hot Gates. The Persian god-emperor Xerxes was on the move with millions of his slave army, set on taking and ruling this world by superior forces.

We got special permission to land down in this book and stories world, old war parallel, and that was what we did. We landed our sleek spaceship down on the Spartan battleplane, and I met with King Leonitus and his queen, Gorgo, being both intelligent and wise. We introduced who we were and explained what we know of the advancing enemy position as well as demonstrated our heavy weaponry. We told him of our security contract and how we were obligated to get all our people out alive, as well as our ship and weaponry, nothing to be left behind. I also spoke of FAE STATE and our connection to this world and its nearby parallels. King Leonitus understood the situation and was grateful for our tactical support.

We arrayed ourselves on the cliffs above the Hot Gates before the three hundred engaged in battle. Our heavy firepower tore through the Persian forces, ripping through three or four people apiece with every machine-gun spray. There were fifty-one of us with five hundred thousand rounds apiece, all tactically equipped. We eradicated millions of the Persians' best and most formidable. Then we were down to five hundred rounds apiece, and I called out our withdrawal. We all jogged back to the spaceship and flew out of this Earth, back into deep space. King Leonitus and his brave king's guard took out thousands more themselves supplemented by a small Athenian militia, before they perished, defending against a massive onslaught.

We reactivated our availability on the security grid network, and everyone asked us where we have been and said that we missed some great ground battles. We showed them video footage of what we were fighting on Earth, and everyone was amazed, wanting to go there themselves and join in the fight. I laughed, as the Spartans were already victorious. The Persians, what was left of their slave armies, broke against the Spartan army, and their emperor, Xerxes, was now dead.

We got new space battle machine guns with full ammunition and weapons depot next time we land for battle. This went on for a long time, for there was always a war to be fought somewhere in some timeline. Eventually, my lovers and companions, the fifty blonde battle babes, parted ways, and I gave them the ship to take back to their home planet with all there many stories and war victories. They were hoping I would be joining them for eternity, but life would lead me elsewhere. It was enough we had these shared experiences as a melded unit, with me as a space battle commander, and so the story unfolds.

No retreat, no surrender; that is Spartan law. And by Spartan law we will stand and fight...and die.

—Spartan Quote

BATTLEFIELD ELVES

In a parallel dimension close by, there was once a massive battlefield dome about the size of a large city. Inside, it had forests and planes and was populated by many different captured species, armed and forced to fight each other for others' entertainment.

Inside, one team was the battlefield elves, armed with heavy-powered machine guns as well as large knives. Pale FAE JAFAE had been dead for some time and could never remember from what, for that time he didn't re-form himself back to life immediately, as he usually did. However, each team had a security console inside the battlefield dome where they could look up and research advanced information about themselves and other species and get communications such as missions, insights, and directives from the people who ran the battlefield dome itself. By the time they brought me back to life as a Pale battlefield FAE, as I was registered on the roster individually, there were only six male battlefield elves left along with two females for a total of eight, after engaging in fierce combat for years against other armed species. This had become their life, and their position was a small forest at the edge of an open grassy plane. They had started with about one hundred elves from their nation that had been captured from spaceships with tractor beams. They were some of the strongest and most intelligent elves I had ever met. The owner of the battlefield dome looked me up and suggested to the battlefield elves to add me to their military unit as a compatible battlefield FAE, knowing that I could be brought back to life and that I had many skills that could be utilized, even outside of combat. And this they did, having first built a Pale FAE combat avatar for JAFAE, personalized for his specific specs, a perfect design, and then activated me back to life with a massive energy surge in the form of a black, gold, and purple lightning bolt.

Among the battlefield elves, I was a completely complementary species as Pale battlefield FAE and got along well with the elves in our forest perimeter. Among the survivors, there was one female elf who was their leader. I called her Elf woman, and she became my mentor and lover. She showed me the security console and eventually let me use it on my own, looking up information about myself, history, and species characteristics of the Pale FAE. We engaged in combat many times, and I and the battlefield elves eliminated all enemy opponents that we were matched up against. In heavy fighting, we charged, yelled, and blasted away with our high-powered machine guns ripping through our alien enemies and racking up many kills.

Eventually, the battlefield dome owner, interested in me specifically and complemented my combat skills, contacted me through the security console. He offered me a chance to trade security technician tactical work in exchange for easier battles and better tips on other enemy locations inside the dome. I talked with elf woman and the other battlefield elves about what an opportunity this was and what it could mean for our way of life, meager as it is between continued fights. The dome owner started me with security camera maintenance all throughout the battlefield dome, and the elves were told to spread out and guard me while I work in each location. We got to do this instead of dangerous fighting often, and it was an easier way of life. I could fly and levitate, so I could reach the cameras all over the battlefield dome. The owner of the dome was grateful for my special skills and the quality of work that I did. He also knew that I was a nobleman and a FAE Elder and that I didn't belong captive in the arena forever, so he made me a deal. He offered me choice to work in combat positions or secret intelligence or my eventual freedom if I work full time for him as a security technician tactical, both technically and tactically, which both he needed. He also assigned two more Pale FAE to our unit, who he had captured from elsewhere, boosting our team's numbers, mixed media, elves, and FAE.

I liked them both instantly, and one told me he was a former admiral of a massive fleet before he was captured by a spaceship. He's much smaller than me and couldn't fly or levitate and told me how scared he was having lost everything he had ever known, along with his position of prestige as an admiral. I felt sorry for him and for everyone in my unit having been captured and forced to fight in life-and-death combat. So I contacted the owner on the security console and told him I would stay and work longer with all my skills in exchange for the freedom of the other Pale FAE and the remaining elves. The owner agreed to the trade, losing nothing and wanting to please me.

Life went on, and I performed a lot of security maintenance as well as occasional battles. We lived on the edge of the forest, and I always said, "I'm with the elves, and we fight for the trees." It made me smile to say it and the elf woman too, before I bend her over and fuck her wet puss from behind as she moaned and orgasmed over and over. As she was our leader, I made sure she was well pleasured. Elf woman constantly researched information on the security console equipped with a vast database and talked to me often about what she learned and discovered. She looked up my personal record often and would tell me I haven't finished my childhood yet as FAE. So after we got special permission from the owner and combat passed, I shape-shifted into a small child self for a little while each day. Elf woman would take me by the hand, and we would walk around the battle-field perimeter of the forest. I thought to myself, *How dangerous it seems where we live together, perceiving danger so differently as an adult Pale FAE.* She would make an Ogham pudding, cradle me, and have me suckle it off her hard nipples and breasts each day, and I would always obey and greatly enjoy this shared activity together.

The two female elves were issued handguns and knives, the male elves had heavy machine guns, the two other Pale FAE were given handguns, and I was equipped with two handheld small machine guns to shoot down enemies from above, being able to fly. In our next two battles, we lost both other Pale FAE, one an admiral, per-ishing under the gunfire of ferocious Orcs, beasts as they were. After this, I got angry and talked to the battlefield dome owner through the security console, telling him I wanted out of the arena with the battlefield elves still alive and well, especially the elf woman. The owner didn't respond; in the meantime, we didn't have to fight, and we relaxed in our forest but always prepared and armed just in case. Eventually, we got a response and a trade option for our immediate release and freedom.

The battlefield dome owner asked me, "Do you remember that you are a FAEmosis and also FAEJA and that you are able to shape-shift as female as well?" At first I didn't and then did when he mentioned it, having forgotten much about myself after dying and being gone for so long the last time. He said that if I fuck him as FAEJA and leave the battle avatar he created for me behind, then we would all be released and free to go, the nine of us. I immediately agreed and wrote him back, thinking what good fortune that was. Elf woman also agreed laughing and saying she would do it herself for freedom from this death pit.

The owner had me escorted by his security guards to a region of the dome I had never been to, exited through a secret door, and then brought to a waiting lounge and eventually his office, meeting him face to face for the first time. He had brown hair and blue eyes and a charming smile. He reminded me that he never captured me and brought me back to life, how I was his favorite champion, and how my skills as a security technician tactical were the best he'd ever seen. I thanked him and appreciated the relationship we've cultivated, although I thought what he did was wrong. We talked for a long while, and he was very polite and respectful and was genuinely interested in me. Then he told me, "It's time for our deal and to shape-shift into FAEJA, your female manifestation," so I did. We fucked in another room, a private suite with a bed. I straddled him, his cock sliding smoothly into my hot puss. My Pale FAE body was naked and my breasts exposed. I rode him for a long time until he came inside of me, very pleased with himself. Then he had me shape-shift back into JAFAE saying he wanted to talk business.

The owner knew I know about and create avatars myself. He asked me what I thought of his creation, of my current vessel, the body housing my spirit and mind consciousness, as I travelled through physical form. I told him, "I'm impressed, and it's better than the ones I can create myself or have tried out before from others."

"In exchange for my avatar technology, your personalized avatar, and all the video security footage of you and the battlefield elves from your time in the dome, I'll trade you," he said.

"For what?" I asked in curiosity.

He said, "For annual security technician tactical work. You're the best there is and have the highest rating. Plus, you can fly and levitate and can reach the cameras high up for maintenance, installation, and replacement. And I can use you tactically to clean out unresponsive combat units hiding in the battlefield dome. Not to mention, I'll save a ton of money having you do this type of work. Plus, each time, I'll have you to fuck me as FAEJA, riding me on top. That's my favorite sex position. In addition, I want you to do security technician work as FAEJA so I can watch and observe you in that way too, but no dangerous tactical cleanouts as her. What do you say? Do we have an agreement?"

I paused to consider and then smiled having decided on the deal. "Yes," I said, "we have an agreement."

"Then you're free to go, and I'll contact you on the security grid when I need you for your skillsets."

We shook hands, and I left being escorted by armed security personnel back to the waiting battlefield elves. I hugged elf woman and picked her up and spun her around, laughing aloud. "We're free," I told everyone. "We can leave now." Everyone tapped my shoulder in good will, smiling together for our freedom and having survived the battlefield dome, which only a few do.

The nine of us were escorted to a different region of the dome we have never been to, and the security guard opened a small door, where we exited, free at last. I stayed and travelled with the battlefield elves for a long time, and then we eventually parted ways, life taking us in different directions. Elf woman eventually became a queen of another elf nation, and the male elves stuck by her side. Many times, I would return to the battlefield dome until my service contract was up, both as FAEJA and JAFAE, in our Pale FAE form and identity. I still thought what the owner did was controversial and wrong,

capturing so many different species from their homelands and forcing them to fight for entertainment. He knew how I felt but always
treated me with the highest respect and was happy to see me when I'd
return for security technician tactical work.

FAE PRIME

F AE Prime and Sister Elf were three planets in the farthest distance of our vast multiverse, all supporting and sustaining intelligent life. FAE Prime glowed pale white in the dark cosmos as the two planets were twinned and had a crossover parallel for travel between them. Sister Elf, the largest by far, glowed bright green, surrounded by the dark matter of deep space.

The Pale FAE of FAE Prime had a small mixed population of both male and female, as well as special forces of military bases and equipment. JAFAE and FAEJA had a small palace on FAE Prime as JAFAE was the owner of the dual planets. JAFAE the Arch admiral personally trained his redcoat special forces, one thousand commanders on FAE Prime, and had them stationed there long term before they were redeployed. Of the one thousand, four were attack helicopter pilots, and four were sharp-toothed predator Pale FAE, which could fly and levitate. This comprised our small air force. Everyone trained on FAE tanks and armored personnel carriers as well as military jeeps. Everyone was issued a FAE machine gun and trained on FAE bazookas. All the commanders in training did additional training as a security tactical as well, with JAFAE being one of the highest-rated security technician tactical himself. After the redcoat special forces commander training, FAEJA, with orange hair and glowing green eyes in her Elven manifestation as Nevele, mated with everyone individually, having them penetrate her in her wet puss from behind. The four sharp-toothed predators entered her ass from behind, guiding their cock inside her with her hand. That was an experience unique to its own. The top chosen hundreds, the cream of the crop, were stationed at the palace. There FAEJA had them lay on the ground and mounted them each apiece riding their pale cocks on top of them until they would come deep inside of her, mating with them for the second time.

Many male Pale FAE, even those living for thousands to trillions of years, never had sex once in their lifetimes and would die virgins or only would try it a few times. But JAFAE wanted his redcoat commanders trained differently. For good morale, she wanted them rewarded for their long-term service, through eternity, as part of FAE STATE military.

Sister Elf was a large elf nation ruled by a young elf queen. They had a large military and modest space fleet with territorial defense and transport ships. Both Pale FAE and the elves can survive in atmospheres of each other's planets, but each preferred their own long term. FAE Prime was desolate and empty of civilization for the longest of times before JAFAE was deeded over the planets and paid the proper fees. Then he added in military and civilian infrastructure and trained his famous one thousand Pale FAE special force commanders. Before this, the Elven military from the Sister Elf planet would send a transport carrier for a few hours of space flight to land down on the surface of FAE Prime for reconnaissance and patrols. That was until JAFAE moved his people in with a FAE STATE contract.

After everything was settled and JAFAE had surveyed the twin FAE planets and experienced traveling through the traverse parallel between the two pale planets, he envisioned his new installations and how he would go about using his designs (he was already a FAE architect) to build fortifications and housing. Next, he flew from FAE Prime over to the glowing green planet of Sister Elf, as some Pale FAE were known to fly through space. He flew into the main Elven city where many elves were gathered while the beautiful and intelligent young elf queen was holding court, and that's when JAFAE introduced himself and said he was moving into the twin planets next store as king. He also brokered an inter-species and planetary alliance between his Pale FAE and the queen's elves, promising to add a space fleet in the future to enhance border security in that far-off region of space and supplement the elves' own formidable space fleet. (JAFAE had already designed and built advanced spacecraft weaponry, which have been tried and tested through Otherworld Defense.) By the end of their meeting, JAFAE being a high-ranking nobleman and Elder, brokered a marriage contract with the young and beautiful elf queen to be fulfilled in the future when he is finished with his undercover missions and deployment elsewhere and then he would return to FAE Prime and Sister Elf.

FAE Christianity

In the beginning was the Source Origin…
And the Elder FAE, Treefolk, Elven lineage from
which it came…
And the Holy Spirit within us all our Sacred
Hearts Aflame…
Together we pray A-FAE

Your each and every Thought, Word, and Action
are your basic creational toolkit. Your every
thought, word, and deed.
You are the full totality of all the lives you have
ever lived. The full totality of your every
Thought, Word, and Action. All combined.
Planting seeds of consciousness in the fertile gar-
dens of the mind, taking root and sprout-
ing, flowing forth it thrives.
FAE perceptions and possibilities enhanced and
restored from the Elder lineage.
There's a new horizon brewing, a fresh perspective restored. A new day arising.

ARCHCARDINAL ORENDA

A rchcardinal Orenda had a wand of pure transfiguration and a clever mind to use it. He could reimagine someone in a moment and recreate them in an instant.

Vatican inquisitor and detective and FAE STATE operative Archcardinal Orenda was known to be Elven and travelled to many parallel worlds as clergy on FAE STATE missions in his purple-blue cardinal robes.

Archcardinal Orenda led the revolutionary war as battle commander and used FAE STATE jurisdiction to unite territories and colonies to form the United States. He also handstitched the first American flags. Shadow histories long forgotten, newly remembered, and partially restored.

He was an excellent sniper and natural leader, especially in battle and with religion. He was FAE Christian. There was much more to be said about Archcardinal Orenda as both cardinal and how he used shadow tactics to win the revolutionary war, but that's for later, still yet to be read. His story goes beyond just Elven lore and legend. He was of French and German elf nobility, being European.

A-FAE we pray this night, by candlelight, casting shadows, and illuminating the darkness.

THE CRUSADES

Sacred hearts aflame ignited and delighted

We forged forward along this lifelong journey, battle ready, defending the realm united and guided under our holy banners flapping in the wind.

We knew. Our spies and operatives told us so. Over the edge of our border and through the heathen lands, they traveled the trade route through Islamist territories. Of those who survived the journey, six of our best spies made it back. Their message and intelligence gathering were the same. Over the edge of our border lie an enemy fortress, one of many, along a trade route of many fortified outposts, eventually leading to a giant walled city with their main forces protected.

The raids and attacks over the border were increasing with ferocious regularity. We knew what to do: it was time to exterminate the wicked foe, stopping them before they could launch their armies against us. So cardinal JAFAE allied all of Christendom, traveling throughout Europe, gathering momentum and military support and pledges from nobles and knights and soldiers to defend the realm and prepare for an all-out organized attack.

Pale FAE JAFAE the Elder led to victory the first and fourth crusade himself as battle commander levitating in the air above the amassed columns and ranks of the many armies rallied and deployed. Among those enlisted were twenty battle saints of old, some brought back to life for the battle to unfold and led the column of holy soldiers arrayed, with black half masks, swords, and pistols.

After the troops were gathered, Cardinal JAFAE was quietly asked if he would serve as pope again, but he insisted on leading the defense response, guiding the armies as battle commander. So the Elven Archcardinal Orenda stayed behind to keep an eye on developments at the Vatican in Italy, although he wished he could deploy and fight the enemy strongholds.

The hidden shadow histories of a long-forgotten era from a long-ago age were barely remembered and largely obscured. A Sacred Heart Crusader and battle saint as well as the creator of FAE Christianity, long before the first crusade, for ten thousand years, Pope JAFAE the Elder reigned from the papal throne of the Vatican. He was the first pope of this world. He was a cardinal of the FAE FAITH, the very first religion. Merging FAE FAITH with Christianity gave us FAE Christianity, and JAFAE led the way. Today, in honor of the memory and lineage, we pray A-FAE!

We used the same strategy each time. Shadow tactics were issued forth from the battle commander who watched and levitated in the air, making sure it was he himself, Pale FAE JAFAE, with his sharp teeth, which was prominent in all his weaponized men's mind's eye. We showed no mercy, no one was raped, and no prisoners were taken. We would post up outside of each fortress stronghold with the majority of our armies in reserve and keeping watch, overwhelming each stronghold we encountered with our attack units and siege ladders. JAFAE would use his FAE majick to take down defenders on the wall from the air as well as hack away with his FAE chopper, a very large sword used aerially, scaring the enemy soldiers and making them abandon their positions over and over.

We had minimal losses and less casualties than planned by the time we reached their main walled city, just as our operatives shared in their reports. We laid siege and broke through their defenses. We took the city destroying their army, guards, and civilian population. Next, the soldiers took other cities we found as well, having trekked so deep into enemy territory. Afterward, all the treasure and valuable items were split up among the nobles, knights, and soldiers. These were the spoils of war, and profitable it was, especially as we lost a few of our numbers among all assembled, our European forces.

The realm was protected, and the first crusade was an easy victory against the Islamic people. Many stayed and occupied the territories acquired, creating crusader cities and outposts. The rest of us returned home eager to be back in our homelands. Some thought the lands were holy, but we viewed them mostly as terrorist-breeding grounds. I reported back to the Vatican our victory and strategies used, first finding the Archcardinal Orenda and the other FAE Christian cardinals among the clergy, as well as the Shadow Conclave, sharing updated reports.

Ever ready, we prepared to defend and deploy against the enemy lands and their dangerous ideologies, always watchful the FAE perceive through their hidden parallels, ready to alert their mortal neighbors to imminent terrorist attacks in the developed world.

A WIZARD'S AMBUSH

The wizarding court of England has summoned the Archcardinal Orenda and a cardinal delegation from the Vatican, but we sensed a trap (you can never trust a wizard, never mind a large group of them). But we must represent ourselves and show no fear even though we recognized no legitimacy or jurisdiction from their wizarding court.

So Archcardinal Orenda selected an elite delegation of cardinals, including two Treefolk shadow cardinals carrying heavy machine guns, fully loaded; two Pale FAE archcardinals who could fly and levitate and were well practiced with battle majick; another two shadow cardinals, vampires both this time, to whom he slipped a handgun apiece for good measure; and the Elven Archcardinal Orenda himself equipped with battle majick, deciding to leave behind his wand of pure transfiguration safe in the Vatican archives.

When they arrived in England and entered the building where the wizards hold court, they knew it was a trap, but they were well prepared and tactically ready. With their cardinal warding abilities, they dampened the wizards' wands, weakening their powers and leveraging a surprise advantage. These weren't weak cardinals, as everyone was battle tested. These were FAE Christians, and they had been directly challenged and their lives threatened.

Walking in, everyone knew the plan. The two Treefolk shadow cardinals were to hold the back entrance with their big bulky bodies and machine guns, keeping their ammunition in reserve and an escape route open if need be. The two vampire shadow cardinals took the lead, pulling out their handguns from underneath their robes and opening fire point blank at the throng of wizards at the front. Once they ran out of ammo, they tossed their guns to the side and moved with super speed, ripping out throat after throat of each target they reached. Eventually, they hit battle frenzy mode and started biting wizards in the neck with their fangs to drain them.

Fast and strong, the wizards were no physical match to the vampires. Next was Archcardinal Orenda who was using battle majick to obliterate his opponents, focusing on the wizard judicials themselves who orchestrated this entire takedown attempt. FAEJA appeared in Pale FAE form teleporting in with a pink plasma orb hovering above one of the palms of her hand. She quickly decided who to vaporize and threw it at a powerful wizard lord about to use his wand and having entered unexpectedly from a side door, about to take aim at Archcardinal Orenda. The pink plasma sphere erased his entire timeline and any future potential for reincarnation. Then she quickly teleported out. The two Pale FAE archcardinals levitated high into the air and took over the center of the room. They used FAE battle majick and, with arcane hand gestures, exploded the heads of each wizard they focused in on, each after the next, whoever grabbed their attention. We killed about one hundred wizards and their judicials all in their stronghold territory, the inner sanctum of their wizard court. Not a one hit us with their wizarding wand blasts. We took out everyone inside. But we knew there were more waiting.

We gathered ourselves and headed for the idle exit door, pushing forward and moving on from the confines of the courthouse. Stepping outside into the fresh night air after these recent kills felt invigorating, and we were ready for whatever forces they had left.

Two hundred English wizards waited outside with wands drawn, utterly perplexed that it was the cardinal delegation exiting the side doors and not their fellow wizard conspirators. Archcardinal Orenda yelled to the two Treefolk shadow cardinals, "Do those machine guns even work? Wipe them out!" Stepping forward and with a guttural growl, the Treefolk opened fire, mowing down every wizard in their path. Not one got a wand blast off as they were so taken by surprise. The battle was won. The seven cardinals, plus FAEJA, mixed media, species, and weaponry, took out three hundred of England's strongest and most troublesome wizards in a short night's work.

Immediately that night, we marched to the Archbishop of Canterbury to make an official clergy report. We arrived, and he was in shock, proclaiming we should all be dead already and not here bothering him. The fool of a mortal, Archcardinal Orenda cut his throat for being in on it, dropping his corpse like the trash he was. Seizing control of the archbishop's vacant position and with his elven cleverness, Orenda switched back jurisdiction of religion back to the Vatican instead of England being independent on rule and record. They maintained their position for some time and then made their way back to Vatican City in Italy to report on their findings and the epic wizard battle they all left unscathed and victorious.

After, Archcardinal Orenda got word from his intelligence network through the Christian church details of the wizards' ambush ambitions and just how far they really went. First, they planned on killing Archcardinal Orenda himself and whatever other elite cardinals he brought with him in the first murder attempt. Next, they kept summoning to wizard court each prominent and powerful cardinal, killing them off each time. Then they planned on marching on the Vatican itself, forcing their way in and taking it over as a wizarding country of their own, an ultimate dream for them. Then they planned to make the Archbishop of Canterbury their puppet pope to help them by ruling the religious right with their wizarding laws, judicials, and lords and manipulating the people. However, their plot was foiled and reported upon after the battle.

Yet another tale of the infamous Archcardinal James Orenda, Elven as he was.

1588

England

Long before Europe was created and set down in this bat-tle-blender books and stories world, England existed having been created by Pale FAE psychologist-architects. They created the mortals who lived in our Earth's realm and the Elder Pale FAE, flying sharp-toothed predators that lived in the FAE parallel next to gray London. They crossed over often or once.

These Pale FAE, the English FAE, mastered space travel early on. They created massive shadow black spaceships with mega plasma blaster rifles and traveled through the far outs of deep space. They conquered alien fleet after alien fleet and many hostile strongholds in far-off dimensions and domains. They annihilated whole existences. They were all war veterans. They then retired their space fleets and plasma blaster rifles, keeping them if they ever needed them again for a later age. They preferred their daggers most of the time and stock-piled kryptonite weaponry.

At some point, the Pale FAE English contacted me in Germany and told me about their whole creation story and about their many space battles and avatar development. They showed the FAE side of things next to our gray England. They said they have seen me in future visions and in past video security footages and knew I was a guardian protector of this multiverse and that they knew I had cho-sen the Pale FAE as one of the four guardian archetypes of our multi-verse, being one as JAFAE myself. Sometimes, we would report intel-ligence information to one another, FAE business, and they respected the work that I did for FAE STATE but were an independent nation of Pale FAE nobility, being English.

The Pale FAE of England went on to teach the mortals their language, FAE script English, often reserved for rare nobility up until this point, as well as their number system and many concepts such as contracts and proper rules and culture. They also shared sacred holidays and rituals. There were other nearby parallels next to England as well; one led to the fairy courts, the others diverse and dangerous, where one should never go into for possibility of never returning.

The year was 1588, and I was residing temporarily in a parallel gray England in our Earth's realm, in the FAE other side of reality. One of my FAE familiars crossed over, a FAE STATE operative, and told me of an imminent invasion by the maritime superpower Spain. They had a massive armada with many ships, a vast fleet of one hundred and thirty filled with sailors, soldiers, and priests for conversion. This was long before England became the vast superpower of the day with its redcoat soldiers and their own armadas. They only had a small navy consisting of much smaller ships, nullifying their ability to ram and sink the much larger Spanish fleet. Also, they were vastly outnumbered by military soldiers for fighting ship to ship, boarding and attacking, hand-to-hand combat, swords and knives, and guns. Their plan was to conquer England outright, overwhelm them with superior numbers, Catholic priests, and soldiers, after landing on the shores. Next, they planned to take Scotland easily and then Ireland, killing everyone on the island and creating another Spanish colony. From there they would parlay with the rest of Europe, sailing instead to North America and claiming the current United States and Canada on old Pandora as Spanish colonies like South America, brainwashing everyone, and forcing their language and religion upon each and every person they leave alive for cooperating with them. I saw this future vision alongside the English Pale FAE in the next door parallel.

Crossing between worlds, I reentered gray England and knew exactly what to do. I levitated up into the air as Pale FAE JAFAE, summoning my weather majick and creating vast storm clouds. I began to attack the oncoming Spanish armada just nautical miles away from the shores of England. With rain, wind, hail, waves, and lightning, I sank each and every ship. None survived the onslaught as I assailed the enemy with the majickal storm and sea arising smashing each ship, drowning all aboard, and stopping their conquistador invasion outright. JAFAE and the Pale FAE saved the day and protected the sovereignty, language, and culture to remain independent in England.

HOW THE REVOLUTIONARY
WAR WAS WON

I n a flash, I saw and knew the future and the potential that I
would activate and the shadow tactics I would utilize to take
us there, together restored and renewed, a vision of the United
States.

This was what I told them, "You will never hold your colonies
without our Pale FAE special forces." Laughing at us and stripping
away uniforms of my redcoat officers and soldiers in dishonor, the
three hundred veterans or so of us left alive of the FAE variety, especially after all the long wars and sea voyages I had led and won as a
redcoat arch admiral, the highest-ranking officer in the British realm.
To make matters worse, we were banished from the domain of the
empire that we had so deeply helped forge and sculpt. Being French
and German helped, but nevertheless, we were disgraced and dishon-
ored after our steadfast service because of our influence, intelligence,
and superior fighting capacity, as well as our FAE powers.

"You will never hold the colonies without the Pale FAE special
forces," Archadmiral JAFAE said one last time over his shoulder with
a dismissive laughter, having already decided what the future was
going to be and how best to achieve it in his mind eye's vison. So
he summoned up the Elven Archcardinal James Orenda in his purple-blue cardinal robe and sleek modernized sniper rifle.

After arriving from the Vatican, JAFAE clued in Archcardinal
Orenda the Elf and FAE STATE private sector representative that he
would start and lead the revolutionary war to victory as battle com-

mander, especially with the growing discontent, overtaxation, and control of the many colonies.

With JAFAE's private sector, FAE STATE, and Archcardinal Orenda a leading representative outfitted with Shadow tactics and ambush strategies alongside the formation of the woods militias, using scarecrow psychology, and the formation of the blue coat regulars under General George Washington.

The war would be won but slightly different than the history we now remember: with a secret French and Vatican alliance, FAE STATE funding, battle strategies, and advanced training, coupled with inside psychology and military knowledge of exactly how the redcoat military operated, which was the biggest superpower of the era, let us not forget, need we remember, and I will remind you, again and again, but yes, oh yes, how did we specifically defeat all the redcoat armies with those clever shadow tactics? With ambush tactics you see.

We collected all the redcoat uniforms from all the dead soldiers and officers and stuffed them with hay, creating scarecrow soldiers by the thousands, all poled and arrayed in perfect formation at the far-edge sight's view of a spyglass or monocular. So the redcoats you see would view it as safe passage to saunter forward toward an already militarily fortified position with their own already deployed troops. With scarecrow psychology, we led them into an ambush—trap. By the time they got close enough to realize the scarecrows weren't their well-positioned comrades, we had Archcardinal Orenda use his Elven sniper rifle to eliminate all the officers in each approaching army, one after the next. It was an easy shot for the Archcardinal to take out the officers. Then our well-trained and uniformed bluecoat regulars would charge forward in front of the arrayed redcoats, shoot twice each, and then run as fast as they could in the opposite direction on cue each time.

After the officers were all dead and the bluecoat regulars had shot and ran from a much larger army, the men would each time dejectedly and, without leadership to command them, start the long walk back to the ships they came in on.

This was when the woods militia would have six rifles apiece loaded and lined up along the tree line, and there were thousands of woods militia. Having waited and watched from the woods the entire time, the enemy was marching in. They knew what to do when they started retreating out and would open fire and wipe everyone out. Each new victory gave us more weapons and ammunition, more redcoat uniforms for scarecrow soldiers, and whatever supplies we found.

Next was our Christmas river attack army to army, our first and most essential to test our strength and route them one on one. While the British position was drunk, reveling, and asleep, I, JAFAE, convinced General Washington to attack and bring out the fighting spirit of victory in him, cleansing him of his moral dilemma. Archcardinal Orenda talked with all the officers and men, telling them to prepare for an imminent Christmas attack and that it was essential we won, especially as we were exposing our main mobilized force, our blue-coat army. We stealthily glided down the river to reach the opposed position, and with drawn sabers glinting, we slashed and stabbed and took down their forces just right, allowing just enough to escape to bring the story back to England, the tales of their continued defeat in the colonies. Not long after, Great Britain formally surrendered.

FAE STATE created the US military and the provided legal jurisdiction to unite colonies and territories to create the United States after the revolutionary war was won and Great Britain accepted defeat.

JAFAE himself painted a priceless famous painting of Archcardinal Orenda and Besty Ross hand-stitching the first American flag that was patented and designed for the Republic for which it stands. Archcardinal Orenda, being Elven and a professional cloak maker, had a stack of one hundred, while old Betsy was working on her famous first flag, alongside General George at the forefront looking on into the distance, while JAFAE was rendering the painting.

After the war, everyone knew General Washington became the first president. He was never a politician but a military officer. Also, little less known, Archcardinal Orenda became the precept of the newly formed United States, finding his own place in the newly minted government. A precept uses preception to look into future potentials and variations of a chosen country. Archcardinal Orenda signed on as precept for over a hundred years and looked toward the future for security and defense as well as FAE STATE business opportunities, which would later come into play. The other founding fathers, a short while longer they would still live, were enthralled that the country would last so long into the future and would grow and grow to become both a military and economic superpower in a far-off modern era.

> *To be prepared for war is one of the most*
> *effective means of preserving peace.*

—George Washington

AMERICAN FAE

I was once a lead musician in a rock band—a singer! I, JAFAE, and three other Pale FAE Parisians, females from France, performed and made records in Europe and then toured the United States once I put together gigs at many different venues. Our music had since been banned. It was chilling and moving and touched and stirred the spirit within, with the sounds of the songs vibrationally emitted.

We toured in our rented navy-blue van with the instruments in the back, the four of us. There was a sleeping pad for two to lie down on in the back of the van, and two rode up front. I drove most of the way. We all carried sharp daggers, for we were ambushed by racists in most of our venues, in the back parking lots, although we had great reviews and most people loved our music, especially vampires. We throated and eyed out our attackers and left those shitbags dead on the pavement sometimes between fifteen and thirty. The four of us, JAFAE and the girls, were stronger and faster with our daggers than the ruffian troublemakers were with their assorted weapons and fists, and we survived and continued to play, making our music alive.

Traveling the States in our van and stopping to rest in locations I rented out in between gigs, we would play the blowjob game to pass the time and connect as a group when we weren't traveling or practicing. The blowjob game consisted of three female FAE taking turns sucking my cock, and whoever's mouth I would come in would win the game, and so would I, every time. They loved to swallow, and all three sucked vigorously, competing and wanting the win for themselves.

Once on the tour we were setting up on stage and a would-be assassin snuck in backstage and lunged at me with a sharp knife. Just before he made contact, our female guitarist smashed him in the face with her guitar, crushing it. I slashed his throat quickly once he was immobilized. She sobbed and sobbed that her guitar was ruined, but I told her not to worry and that I was rich and would buy her a new one before our next venue on the tour. I was just so grateful that she had saved my life and our tour. I had her sing with me up front of that gig. I took my time with her that night, rewarding her for saving my life, and we had sweet sex for hours together.

I was a Pale FAE nobleman, and I had to request and be approved to sing publicly and form a band and record music and perform live concerts. In the end, after our American tour, I couldn't decide who I was attracted to more, so I married all three of my bandmates, the drummer and two guitarists. Through marriage, I made all three countesses because I was an Earl. We slept together all the time and fucked regularly. I would mate with them individually. I found them in France as young girls and taught them FAE script English. Then we formed our band, American FAE, and practiced and played music we created; we made it come to life.

I remember thinking over and over how much this country had evolved since I had created it with FAE STATE through the revolutionary war and the solidification of the states once the country and government were formed and recognized globally.

After our long tour, we left this world for a parallel FAE dimension, and they lived out their natural first life incarnation with me married in bliss. The name of our band is the same as the language we speak today in the States—American FAE! And that's my short little story; we were famous musician FAE.

Once upon a time, Elves and FAE and Treefolk
used to live in this world dominantly, not just
here and there and few and far between.

A KANDYLAND STORY

Kandyland was a FAE dimension and superpower equipped with planetary supernukes and populated by Pale FAE redcoat's special forces, Christmas elves, Keebler elves, leprechauns, sharp-toothed cookie monsters, and blue Kandy dwarf dragons.

JAFAE created Kandyland as a psychologist-architect as a Candyland extension strategy. Later, all of Candyland was ceded over to JAFAE and FAE STATE, with the proper jurisdiction and payment accounted for, thus, becoming Kandyland with a K, under Pale FAE special forces redcoat military protectorate. There were also armed Elven militias among the Christmas elves with high-powered firepower. We even handed out handguns to complement the knives of the Keebler elves, and they were skittish. You would never catch one. They would unload one you in seconds. The blue cookie monsters with their sharp teeth flew the Kandy dwarf dragons through the sky, wielding battle maces and practicing battle alchemy. Up until this point, JAFAE had lived in exile from Candyland, although always monitoring developments in one of his favorite world spectrum FAE dimensions and former kingdom homeland.

Once I was the king of Candyland, in a FAE dimension in a childhood incarnation as Pale FAE JAFAE, and I had a Kandy handgun that fired plasma blasts and that I always kept at my side in a holster, having designed, tested, and built it myself. I could levitate and fly and had many candy people as subjects to consider as to their well-being.

One early morning, I was holding court as usual with my guards and populace, a small gathering, when suddenly, about one hundred candy-cane soldiers in green and white uniforms arrived, brandishing swords and charging in our direction. My guards moved to intercept and fought valiantly but were quickly cut down. I immediately unholstered my Kandy blaster handgun and started to fire at the incoming uniformed troops. I took out the first twenty of their best soldiers before I was tackled to the ground and my blaster handgun taken from me. I've been captured and taken prisoner, and all my people were gathered and executed.

"You're to be brought before our high FAE king for judgment," the Tan FAE sharp-toothed candy-cane officer said to me. I was detained and then marched off in the direction the soldiers charged from where I am and was eventually escorted before their high king. The candy-cane king is a Tan FAE sharped-toothed predator with a golden crown atop his head, seated on a throne, surrounded by more green and white uniformed officers and soldiers. The high FAE king, recognizing me as a Pale FAE Elder and nobleman, ordered me exiled, never to return again while he reigned and ruled all of Candyland, which was his childhood dream he told me. He also kept my handgun for himself, as well as my territories. They banished me but spared my life. For this, I was grateful although saddened about living in exile, away from the Candyland dimension, colorful, happy, and bright that I had known as home for so long.

Many trillions of years passed by, but I always checked back and monitored ongoing developments on Candyland with secret security cameras I later installed. But I must get back in, someway, somehow. The worlds called to me, gravitationally pulled me, and drew me in. I know I belong there but lived in exile. They knew who I am; even in my adult form as Pale FAE, they would recognize me in an instant. This was before my redcoat special forces were trained and developed, and I had no armies of my own to retake my lost domain. Plus, it was a high FAE king, so I was not completely upset over the change in ruler.

So I developed a plan to return. I knew I needed to, to maintain my story and vibrational connection to Candyland. But I decided I must go undercover. I've already scoped out the area and monitored a rural plane rarely frequented by the candy-cane patrols. There was an intelligent, yet cleverly dangerous, male Candyland creature I've been watching with growing interest and curiosity. So I shape-shifted into FAEJA as the Elven orange-haired and green-eyed Nevele and put myself on Candyland immunity testing on my female persona for the next decade. I mated with the colorful Candyland creature constantly. He would fuck me from behind or lay me down on my back, spreading my legs wide, all day every day, and candy would come inside of me. But he constantly put candy goo puss tarts inside of my vagina, trying to transfigure me into part of Candyland. My immunity testing held up, and I didn't die and was not transfigured either. We didn't talk much but mate constantly, with vigor. Eventually, my time in Candyland was fulfilled, and Nevele the Elf shape-shifted back into Pale FAE FAEJA and flew away into another story. The high FAE king and his candy-cane soldiers never knew I secretly returned and lived there once again.

Many trillions of years continued to pass by, but I never forgot Candyland and my love for it. Eventually, I patented and designed Kandyland as a FAE psychologist-architect level III and secretly slipped it into the Candyland dimension as future strategy for my long-awaited return from exile.

This brought me to this life, now undercover as a small Tan FAE child pretending to be human or at least mortal FAE in the current United States, going by James or young Jimmy Mullen. This was my weakest incarnation on the pendulum, and I had lost most of my FAE abilities, including shape-shifting for the time being. Spending lots of time at the playground and the Invisible Library beside it, I often talked about being FAE and about other worlds, as well as portal technology with the librarians. They tried to recruit me and mold me as an Invisible Librarian. One day, I said to them, "You know Candyland? It's not just a game for children but a real and very dangerous dimension."

The librarian chuckled and asked me, "How do you know that?"

I told her, "I used to live there. I was once a Kandy king but was defeated in battle and exiled by the high FAE king." They loved my stories and knew they are real. So we made a secret FAE-library alliance. We used to be enemies, and the library rarely worked with the FAE, but they liked me and wanted me for their own. We talked about sympathetic links and how every book held the energy of the stories contained within them, some being rarer and more desired than others, increasing their value. They told me about all the worlds that had libraries and museums and how they were all connected through an interdimensional network, linked one to the next across the many multiverses.

I asked them about the maps of all the worlds and how much they have charted out and if I could see them. But the librarian responded, "Those are the highest classified materials that we have, and it's rare to have access to the whole grid." Even she did not know how deep it all goes. She told me to keep reading and that in some worlds, histories and people and places were real and alive and in other parallel worlds, they were represented in works of fiction, still sharing valuable lessons. She told me to always say I was working on a fiction book so that if anyone ever overheard what I was talking about, I could always write it off as creational brainstorming for a book I was writing. I told her someday I will write a book and add a story of the library in it. She paused and looked shocked and then nodded her head in agreement.

There are other Invisible Library crossover stories that can't be shared at this time and are not pertinent to this particular story. So let's keep on track, shall we? But before we continue, let me share that occasionally, the library got me Pale FAE avatars for off-world missions so I could be JAFAE again for a little while, and FAEJA worked for the library, on under renovation, in Boston for a while while we dive undercover again.

There were nine mutant dominant worlds parallel to the Candyland dimension. These were filled with superheroes and supervillains, and their population worshipped them and their powers, being their world's version of celebrities or logo stars. These worlds also had libraries built within their infrastructure. Occasionally, there was an interdimensional rift, and a school bus or two would end up on Candyland filled with schoolchildren, never to be seen again.

Eventually, being much younger worlds, the superheroes started flying over and attacking the FAE, targeting the candy-cane soldiers stationed there in their green and white uniforms. We hated superheroes; they were the enemy, not all mutants, but the superheroes we despised.

So there was a black-ops mission, and I was telepathically contacted by the library, as they sometimes do regarding FAE business, knowing I had a deep connection with Candyland already from previous lives lived. The superheroes were attacking Candyland, and the high FAE king was declaring war against their nine planets. Also, the librarians on the superhero mutant dominant worlds were no longer responding back to the greater library network, having gone rogue, lost in their own spectrum of existence, rooting for their favorite heroes and villains. So with my approval and shadow tactics and secret support being Kandyland nobility in exile, we formed a plan to open blue portals for the high FAE king to invade the mutant worlds, one after the other. And this we did. The uniformed candy-cane troops assembled with the Candyland terraformer expansionists, wearing thick goggles and having candy-goo backpacks connected to dispersion guns, which would transform the world's physical substrate into Candyland. While the candy-cane troops invaded and slaughtered everyone they came across with their swords and smiles and sharp teeth, the terraformer expansionists quietly began to candy-goo the infrastructure and natural world, turning it into a Candyland extension satellite.

The candy goo colorfully took hold and then began to rapidly expand and grow, overriding everything in its path. This caused chaos, and the superheroes and villains were very disorganized, not prepared for an invasion. The police forces were no match for the ferocity of the candy-cane troops during wartime invasion strategy. Whatever military they had made no difference, and the technology and infrastructure were overridden once the candy goo spread over it. The high FAE king took down five mutant planets and turned them into small Candyland satellite worlds completely, stationing his troops before the war hit a standstill. He couldn't expand anymore and still hold the territories he recently altered and was taken by superior FAE force.

Years passed by, and still Candyland was at war with the mutant superhero worlds. Then, something shifted, and FAE STATE was awarded Candyland to purchase all together, and JAFAE was invited to return. All was to become Kandyland with a K, changing the name and ownership. This included the core worlds beyond the black abyss where all the planetary supernukes were stored, as well as all the denizens of the realm.

Immediately, I deployed my redcoat units, Pale FAE special forces, to Kandyland. The candy-cane soldiers resisted as best they could but were no match for the redcoats. We fought two skirmishes and a big battle, killing off their Tan FAE sharp-toothed soldiers, each and every one. They were in shock at how strong and well-disciplined the redcoats were and how fiercely ferocious. Then quickly we captured the high FAE king with his crown and his throne and his top general with a moustache and monocle.

The orders were to spare the former high FAE king and his top general, leaving his occupying troops on the former mutant worlds alone for now, for once he spared my life as well. The former king begged to stay in Kandyland, saying that it was his favorite place to exist and that it was always his childhood dream to rule, plus complementing himself on his war victories and planetary takeovers. I decided to let him stay, still being away myself, and had him kept under the watchful eye and strong guard of my redcoat soldiers.

Next, we moved more Christmas elf militias and the sharp-toothed Pale FAE duke along with the cookie monster magistrate with his dragon familiar over to where the high FAE king was ruling from, making it the duke's new duchy and giving him command of the ongoing mutant war. He said, "What an honor it is to serve the Shadow Jester, being FAEJA and JAFAE, James and Nevele, Treeja and TreeFAE," knowing I was a former king of Kandyland and that my position with FAE STATE was bigger than that now.

The Christmas elves took the candy-goo backpacks with their dispersion guns and goggles and prepared for an imminent attack on the next mutant world, this time led by Pale FAE special forces, redcoat units. The FAE duke was eager to prove himself and continue the war effort against the enemy. The next four mutant worlds fell, one after the other, quickly and easily defeated; the mutants and their mortals were no match and were crushed in the chaos of battle. These small worlds belonged to Kandyland now, after purchase and Kandy-terraforming.

Next, we were contacted by the Pale FAE deities, the first beings to exist after the Source Coders set their species templates into fresh life. They were the creators of Candyland but had lost most of their control, except a few nuclear-equipped core worlds they still maintained rule of, although FAE STATE had ownership. We were allies, and I was a Pale FAE deity as well; these were my elders, so I respected them and valued their creation of Candyland in the first place, knowing my battles and wars were at the tail end of Elder histories of Kandyland. Long may we reign.

In the next parallel over there is a human delegation, including three hundred planets altogether. They collectively decided to declare war on Kandyland, challenging the FAE duke directly and myself as the Shadow Jester, high liege and owner of FAE STATE. The Christmas elves were put in charge of weapons production and nuclear strategies. I gave the go ahead, and we decided on nuclear first strikes, before they could invade us. The Christmas elves' drone drove every planetary supernuke filled with Kandy goo for atmospheric and terrestrial takeovers through deep space. We were in an all-out war scenario. With the mutant worlds defeated and the human worlds being absorbed with Kandy goo supernukes, our enemies were disappearing one world after another.

"They were fools to declare war on us," the FAE duke said to the sharp-toothed blue cookie monster magistrate, his closest companion.

"Ha ha ha ha ha ha." Laughed the Cookie Monster magistrate. "We will absorb all their worlds for Kandyland, expanding our territories, erasing our enemies, and winning the war."

"All to be expected," replied the Pale FAE duke deep in his duchy, sitting upon the old throne of the former high FAE king.

What happened to him anyway, you may be wondering? The FAE duke had the former king executed for treason alongside his top general with the mustache and monocle. He attempted an overthrow in the absence of the Shadow Jester, thinking he could fool the duke and magistrate and thinking he could get the elves to side over to him.

Then the Pale FAE redcoats, special forces, ambushed the last of the candy-cane soldiers, Tan FAE and sharp-toothed in their green and white uniforms, eliminating the last of the old order and securing the satellite worlds, former mutant strongholds, for FAE STATE.

"Beware of the candy witch from Candyland and her colorful candied gingerbread house. She'll trap and capture you and lock you up in a cage, feeding you candy and cakes until you're plump. Then she'll cook you up in the oven and eat you for dinner. Beware of the candy witch," so says Hansel and Gretel, "Deep in the forest she hides her home."

ALONG THE JOURNEY

Two redcoat officers' special forces on FAE STATE business suddenly came across a giant sphinx, just having been talking about the chances of crossing paths with a colorful fierce and fire-breathing Nogard today (that's a dragon if you didn't know). But they happened to land a sphinx on this extended outward-bound mission.

All levitating in the air, the giant sphinx asked a riddle in order to live on and pass by. "What gives guys? And don't say fruit trees."

The Pale FAE officers responded one and then the other, "The hands that feed."

"The mind that knows and shares."

Passing the test and solving the riddle, the two Pale FAE redcoat officers flew past the enormous and deadly sphinx along their journey. One officer asked the other, and not for the first time, "Where do you think Saint James is these days?"

"The Butcher?" the other redcoat officer responds.

"Yes!" he replied. "Our Archadmiral, FAE STATE military special forces."

"I think he's deep undercover again, back on the Earth's realm, obscured and largely forgotten."

"But not forgotten by us," he said.

"No, never! We're his best veterans!"

"At least it wasn't a Nogard we had to talk with. I would rather take a riddle from a sphinx any day. How many types of dragons do you know of?"

"Well, there are talking FAE dragons, and they tend to be colorful and bright and very intelligent. There's the Archdrakon that can shape-shift from dragon to Drakon form. The Drakon, which are immortals, are spliced with dragon DNA. And the dragons that are more like beasts that can sometimes be tamed and even ridden by dragon riders."

"Well-spoken and well said," responded the other officer.

"But there's one more variety I know of."

"And what's that?" he asked.

"The Asian dragons looking different and without wings that can levitate and portal!"

"Ah, but of course, I never think of them."

Dragons are very diverse and Nogard-like in their behaviors and thinking patterns. They are both fiery ferocious and deadly dangerous. Beware of the ambush predators.

AFTERWARD

It was about vibration and frequency, and the particle-building blocks of life. Templates to contemplate and embody. Sacred forms and blended variations.

And the possibilities of the many-manifest forms that are seen and understood, a grand variety.

I went as far as I could, at the forefront of consciousness. A new perspective enhanced, achieved, and activated.

I've put so many things into play. Thoughts and ideas and revelations.

There are many people and many places that live in parallel worlds beside us, and in the in-betweens. Books and stories and long-forgotten histories tell the tale.

Different facets, different aspects, with varied creations.

There was a way to the story. That it could be told and retold, again and again. Through a developed story-scribe tale.

Source code activation, Source integrity, inherent within.

In this moment in time-space, here in this realm, present and aware, we hear the call. A new day arising.

This world has many histories and shadow histories that have shaped and formed it, over and over, again and again.

Source code activation 11:11 sacred hearts aflame. Beyond the forevers and in-betweens.

Painted light and colored shadows, perceptions and variations. Invested interplay.

There was a time and a place, there was a rhyme and a reason in season to reflect and remember one's true calling and purpose.

There was a tale to be told and a story to be heard, beckoning the recitation to begin.

You've heard it all now...but you never know, there could be a little bit more too as this story is unfolding.

I know for many of you this is new information. But there is a time for integration. To let everything settle in.

Should we sail away, over the horizon and through the in-betweens, through another parallel, a new world beginning, a fresh day, a new dream?

Lest we forget, need we remember, I will remind you, again and again.

It made more sense the more you heard, each new piece unfolding. Telling a story of a tale long told. It's true you knew once you've heard it.

Sometimes, there are doorways between dimensions and different worlds, and sometimes you can cross through and experience a new reality. Within and without.

So there was a potential, a Source code revelation. And so the story unfolds. For those with

a mind to know, fresh perspectives, new perceptions, horizons, and frontiers. Bridging realities
and forming new possibilities. Again, and again.

A-FAE I pray by candlelight to illuminate
the night and cast the shadows.

An Elf on the Shelf

There was an elf on my shelf, and her name was Zelda. I bought her off eBay as a toy figurine. She was beautiful in her wise Elven ways. Princess Zelda was my muse for this FAE STATE story. To have an elf on your shelf is good luck. That's why there's an elf on my shelf today.

ABOUT THE AUTHOR

J ames has always been an avid reader and creative writer. He is a lover of nature and greatly enjoys the outdoors. This book was written while he worked his day job as a cleaner at Bowdoin College. James lives alone on Orrs island in Harpswell Maine.

www.ingramcontent.com/pod-product-compliance
Lightning Source LLC
Chambersburg PA
CBHW031711210125
20607CB00045B/827